For John and Aida, with love and hope. – CB

Dedicated to all the people making a difference for the future of our planet. – SW

For Charlie. With love. — AH

For all of those who tirelessly work to solve climate change. – ML

Quarto Knows

Inspiring | Educating | Creating | Entertaining

Brimming with creative inspiration, how-to projects, and useful information to enrich your everyday life, Quarto Knows is a favourite destination for those pursuing their interests and passions. Visit our site and dig deeper with our books into your area of interest: Quarto Creates, Quarto Cooks, Quarto Homes, Quarto Lives, Quarto Drives, Quarto Explores, Quarto Gifts, or Quarto Kids.

The publishers and authors would like to thank Andrew Simms and Professor Dudley Shallcross for their invaluable advice and support as consultants for this book.

Text © 2021 Catherine Barr and Steve Williams.
Illustrations © 2021 Amy Husband.

First published in 2021 by Frances Lincoln Children's Books, an imprint of The Quarto Group.
The Old Brewery, 6 Blundell Street, London N7 9BH, United Kingdom.
T (0)20 7700 6700 F (0)20 7700 8066 www.QuartoKnows.com

ISBN: 978-0-7112-5628-6

The illustrations were created digitally.
Set in Gill Sans.

Published by Katie Cotton and Georgia Amson-Bradshaw
Designed by Sasha Moxon and Myrto Dimitrakoulia
Edited by Claire Grace and Lucy Menzies
Production by Dawn Cameron

Manufactured in Guangdong, China TT042022

10 9 8 7 6 5 4 3

FSC
www.fsc.org
MIX
Paper from responsible sources
FSC® C016973

The Story of CLIMATE CHANGE

A first book about how we can help save our planet

Catherine Barr and Steve Williams
Illustrated by Amy Husband and Mike Love

Frances Lincoln
Children's Books

Billions of years ago, Earth was very hot.
Rivers of red lava and tumbling black rocks snaked across
a burning globe, while erupting volcanoes spewed clouds
of dust into the sky. Earth's first atmosphere was made of
a swirling mix of poisonous gases that wrapped around it.

Smelly gas

4.5 – 2.3 billion years ago

Over time as temperatures fell, clouds formed and the lava cooled. Icy comets from space crashed and melted on Earth. It started to rain and the planet turned from red and black to blue as new oceans filled up.

Life first formed in these oceans and one day, tiny, blue-green algae used sunlight to grow. This released oxygen and the planet's atmosphere began to change.

O_2

O_2

O_2

In time, as plants flourished, the amount of oxygen in the air grew too. This new gas shielded Earth from the sun's super scorching rays. Animals could now live on land as well as in the water. Life continued to evolve... giant dragonflies rested on ferns, amphibians waded into water and huge scorpions and other bugs scuttled through slippery green forests.

2.3 billion – 300 million years ago

New shoots stretched towards the sun as rotting plants sank into the swamp.
Over millions of years, this cycle of life turned dead plants into coal.

In the seas, dying bacteria, algae and plankton drifted down to the ocean
floor. These tiny life forms got squashed in sand and mud and very slowly
became oil and gas. Along with coal, these are our fossil fuels.

Wow! What
a wingspan!

I'm just too
small to see

Over billions of years, Earth's climate changed in cycles of hot and cold. As the planet baked and froze, more fossil fuels formed.

Nice and warm today

Mostly the climate has been hot. Gases wrapped around the planet, trapping heat like a blanket. Life thrived on this greenhouse-like Earth — from tiny bacteria to tall trees, stomping dinosaurs and blooming flowers.

300 – 65 million years ago

But disaster struck! A huge asteroid crashed into the planet, almost destroying life on Earth. The dinosaurs were plunged into cold darkness as dust billowed all around and blocked out the sun. With nothing to eat, the dinosaurs died... but some life did survive.

Look at that!

Over time, sunlight burned through the dusty haze created by the asteroid collision with Earth.

You were easy to spot

Mammals took over the land and life exploded once again. Over millions of years, humans evolved and explored the world. People learned different skills, gathered knowledge and lived in harmony with nature.

65 million years ago – c.1850s

People discovered how to release energy by burning fossil fuels. Humans began to burn oil, gas and coal and this new energy changed everyone's lives. People could now climb aboard trains, work in busy factories and live in warmer, well-lit homes.

Cough

Cough

That pollution is going to be a problem...

But when fossil fuels burned, a gas called carbon dioxide drifted up into the sky. Levels of this gas in the atmosphere began to rise. In a short time on Earth, humans were already beginning to change the air.

As the world developed, the number of people grew and grew. More land was needed for people to live and farm food. Forests disappeared as trees were cut down to build homes. More and more space was cleared so farmers could plant crops and rear animals like cows and sheep to feed the growing human population.

1850s – modern day

But farm animals add another greenhouse gas called methane to our atmosphere. It mostly comes from cows burping and farting. Like carbon dioxide, methane traps heat on Earth, adding to the greenhouse effect.

where are all the trees?

BURP

BURP

BURP

BURP

This harmful gas also seeps from piles of rotting city waste and melting Arctic bogs. As temperatures across the world rise, frozen bogs soften and bubbles of ancient methane, the size of grapefruits, burst from the warming Earth.

As well as the methane in bogs, scientists are measuring bubbles of ancient air trapped in mountain glaciers and deep polar ice to study the story of climate change.

High on top of a volcano in Hawaii, USA, under bright blue skies, one scientist began to measure carbon dioxide in our air. He plotted a graph which shows carbon dioxide levels rising – trapping more and more heat on planet Earth.

1958 – today

Professor Keeling's graph

This doesn't look good for the planet.

It's going up and up!

Today, the whole world is watching as scientists plot this upward curve. The Keeling Graph shows the speediest climate change in human history.

But what does climate change mean for our planet?
As temperatures rise, oceans soak up the heat which causes seawater to warm. This upsets the balance of nature in our seas. Habitats like coral reefs are dying in warmer waters and all over the world, plants and animals are losing their homes.

Today

As glaciers melt, ice sheets slip faster into the sea, causing sea levels to rise. This makes tides rise further up beaches across the world, threatening eggs laid by shore-nesting creatures like sea turtles. Higher seas flood the land, causing problems for animals and people living on low islands.

My ice is shrinking

Yummy penguins

As polar ice melts, polar bears and penguins struggle to breed and feed because the ice they live on is disappearing. Whales and other sea life eat krill, but these shrimp-like creatures are vanishing as the ice shelves where they live melt away.

As the atmosphere changes, ocean currents are shifting. This changes the weather, making rain, drought and winds more extreme.

Changes to the climate are having a huge impact across the globe. Ferocious hurricanes, spreading drought and shifting rain patterns are changing life on Earth.

In many hot countries, deserts are becoming bigger. Forests are drying out, which sparks raging fires that fill the air with smoke. Seas are warming, coastlines are flooding and storms are surging over land.

Where are my mates?

Where's my forest?

Where are all the fish?

Today

Where's the ice?

Across the world, plants and animals flee or must adapt to this rapid change. Migrating herds of elephants and other animals arrive at dry rivers and water holes, forest monkeys and apes swing away from burning trees and in the Arctic Ocean, exhausted polar bears paddle between melting ice. Only the fittest survive.

Where's my mum?

Climate change is destroying habitats and threatening more and more plants and animals. Many are becoming extinct.

As the climate changes, people are also forced to migrate. Families and communities are escaping drought, rising seas, disease and disappearing homes by abandoning where they live to seek somewhere safer.

Flooding and drought mean that farmers need to look for new land to farm or find different seeds that will grow in changing weather.

Today

Rising seas are lapping closer to coastal cities and towns, flooding people's homes and businesses. As more of the world warms up, mosquitos spread diseases such as malaria to new areas. In crowded cities, health risks rise.

This means that millions of people must walk, ride, fly or sail away from their homes in search of new shelter, safety and food.

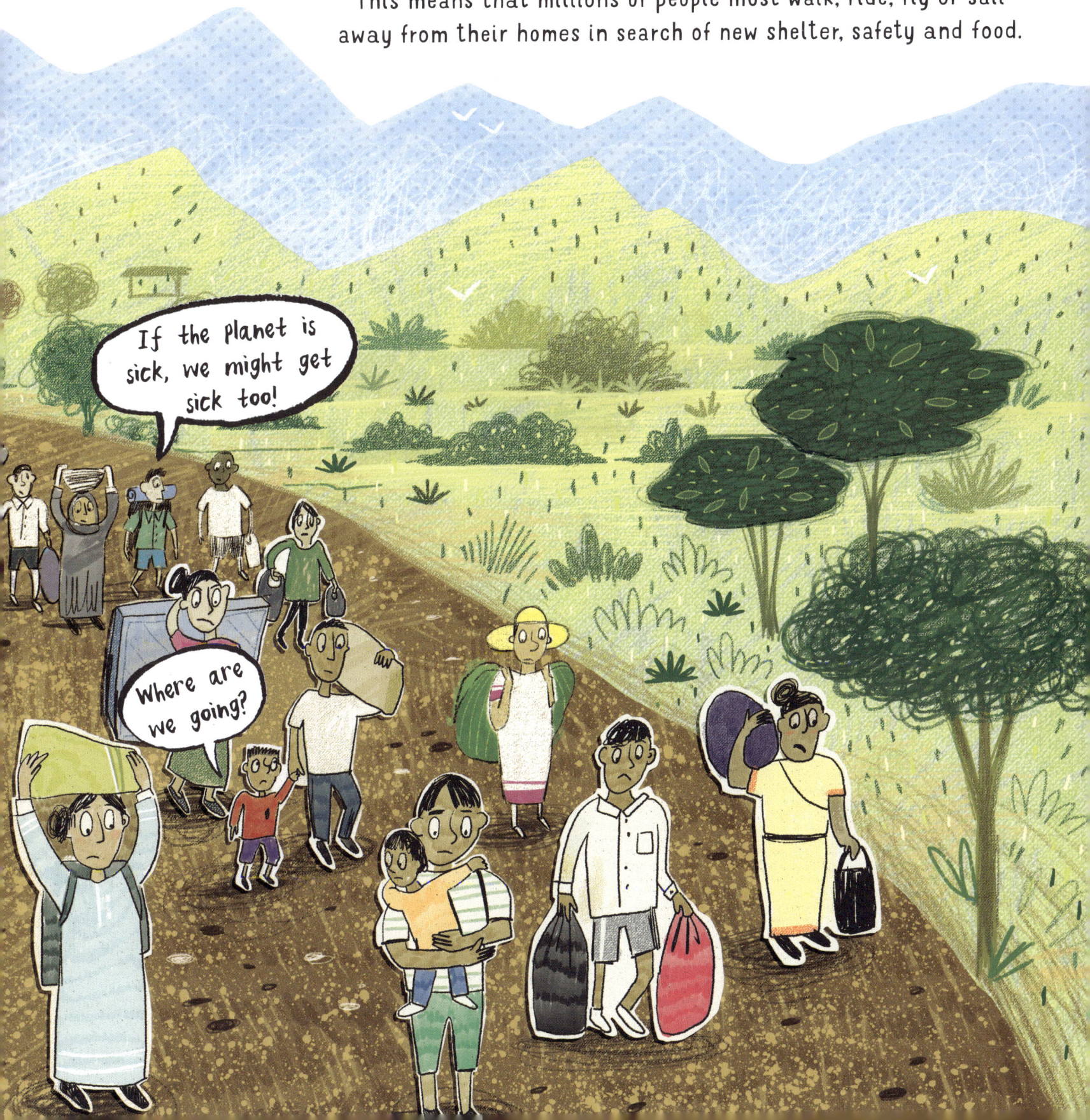

Rich countries burn fossil fuels to release energy and make products like cars that lots of people want. More and more people want these things, which means that forests disappear, people squash into cities for factory jobs and waste piles up.

We used to know when the rains came...

People in poor countries suffer the most from the impact of climate change. While many men move to bustling cities to work, mothers and children look after the farms. They go hungry when crops fail. Drought forces women and girls to walk further to find water, leaving less or no time for school.

Today

When girls do go to school in poor countries, they marry later, have fewer children and bring up healthier families. Educated women have more successful farms which are better able to meet the challenge of climate change. Girl power can change the world!

Who's causing climate change?

From remote glaciers to dark forests, mountain tops, busy cities and deep seas, scientists are measuring the changes taking place on Earth. They have discovered how nature, especially oceans and forests, can help slow down climate change.

Today

In sunlit oceans, billions of tiny floating plants take carbon dioxide from the air and use it to grow. On land, this greenhouse gas is used by trees which store carbon for hundreds of years. But when forests are cut down or burned, carbon drifts back into the air. As oceans warm, they are less able to soak up damaging levels of greenhouse gas from the air.

Such fresh air!

CO_2

CO_2

CO_2

By caring for our oceans and saving our forests, we can help to stop the build-up of greenhouse gases that is causing the world's climate to change.

The Amazon is the biggest rainforest in the world, so it really helps to slow down the effects of climate change. But even this gigantic forest is disappearing. Huge areas of land in the Amazon are stolen from people who have always lived there. This land is cleared for local cattle and crops that also feed farm animals in countries far away.

I'm bored

I'm squashed

Today

Tropical forests in many countries could be saved if everyone everywhere ate less meat. We can tuck into more beans, vegetables and try meat-free alternatives. From plant-based burgers to veggie pies, exciting new food is being developed that tastes delicious, and helps protect forests. It's an important part of the fight against climate change.

Most of the energy that we use still comes from burning fossil fuels. But a new kind of energy is changing the world. Green energy uses the rays of the sun, the power of the wind and the tides and waves. These alternatives are renewable – they can go on forever without polluting Earth.

Today

We use energy every day to travel, make things, turn on lights and heat our homes. But buildings can be made that trap heat and use a lot less energy. From building eco-friendly homes, using bicycles and using alternative fuels, there are plenty of ways to use clean, green power to fight climate change.

Scientists all over the world have proved that humans are causing climate change.

They are gathering facts, sharing knowledge, looking to the future and suggesting how we can stop damaging our Earth.

Millions of children are making their voices heard too by asking brave questions and protesting against the dangers of climate change. These young activists are telling grown-ups that they care about the planet too!

2019 – today

Children and scientists are asking people to choose green energy, support sustainable farming, buy less, waste less and do more to care for nature. This way, we can end the human-made threat to our planet.

Humans have discovered ways to solve the climate emergency. Through our mistakes, we now understand that it's important to treat nature gently, rather than destroy it. We have learnt how to look after the soil, trees and seas and how to protect people, habitats and wildlife.

We are inventing new and better ways to live in harmony with Earth. From world leaders to our own families, it is time for everyone who can to make choices every single day that protect our precious planet.

Plant-based burger coming up!

COOK VEGAN

Today – future

We can all plant trees, eat less meat, buy fewer things, use less energy, create less waste and share climate facts with family and friends. Now it's up to you to write the next chapter in the story of climate change!

Today – future

2019 – today

Glossary of useful words

Atmosphere – the different gases that surround Earth or other planets in outer space.

Asteroid – a lump of rock and metal that orbits the Sun.

Blue-green algae – tiny living things that can make their own food from sunlight and carbon dioxide.

Carbon dioxide (CO_2) – a greenhouse gas that is naturally used by plants to make their own food on Earth. Carbon dioxide is released back into the air when fossil fuels (made from ancient living things) are burned.

Climate change – changes in world weather, most recently caused by human activities such as burning fossil fuels.

Climate emergency – a changing global climate that threatens the survival of most life on Earth.

Comet – a ball of ice, rock and dust in space.

Evolution – the way in which living things change over time, sometimes into new kinds of life.

Extinction – the dying out or disappearance forever of a type of living thing.

65 million years ago

65 million years ago – c.1850s

1850s – modern day

1958 – today

Today

Today

Fossil fuels – natural fuels made from fossilised plants and animals, for example, coal, oil and natural gas.

Greenhouse effect – the warming of Earth by gases, like carbon dioxide and methane, that trap heat in Earth's atmosphere.

Greenhouse gas – any gas in our atmosphere that traps the sun's heat on Earth and contributes to global warming.

Methane – a greenhouse gas. Most methane in Earth's atmosphere is now created by human activities.

Migration – the movement of any living thing, including people, to find suitable conditions for life.

Oxygen (O_2) – a gas with no colour or smell that is made by plants. Most living things need to breathe oxygen to stay alive.

Plankton – mostly microscopic plants and animals that live in fresh or salt water.

Renewable energy – energy from resources like sun, wind and water that nature can replace.

Sustainable – using natural resources in a way that allows time for these resources to replenish and does not damage the natural world.

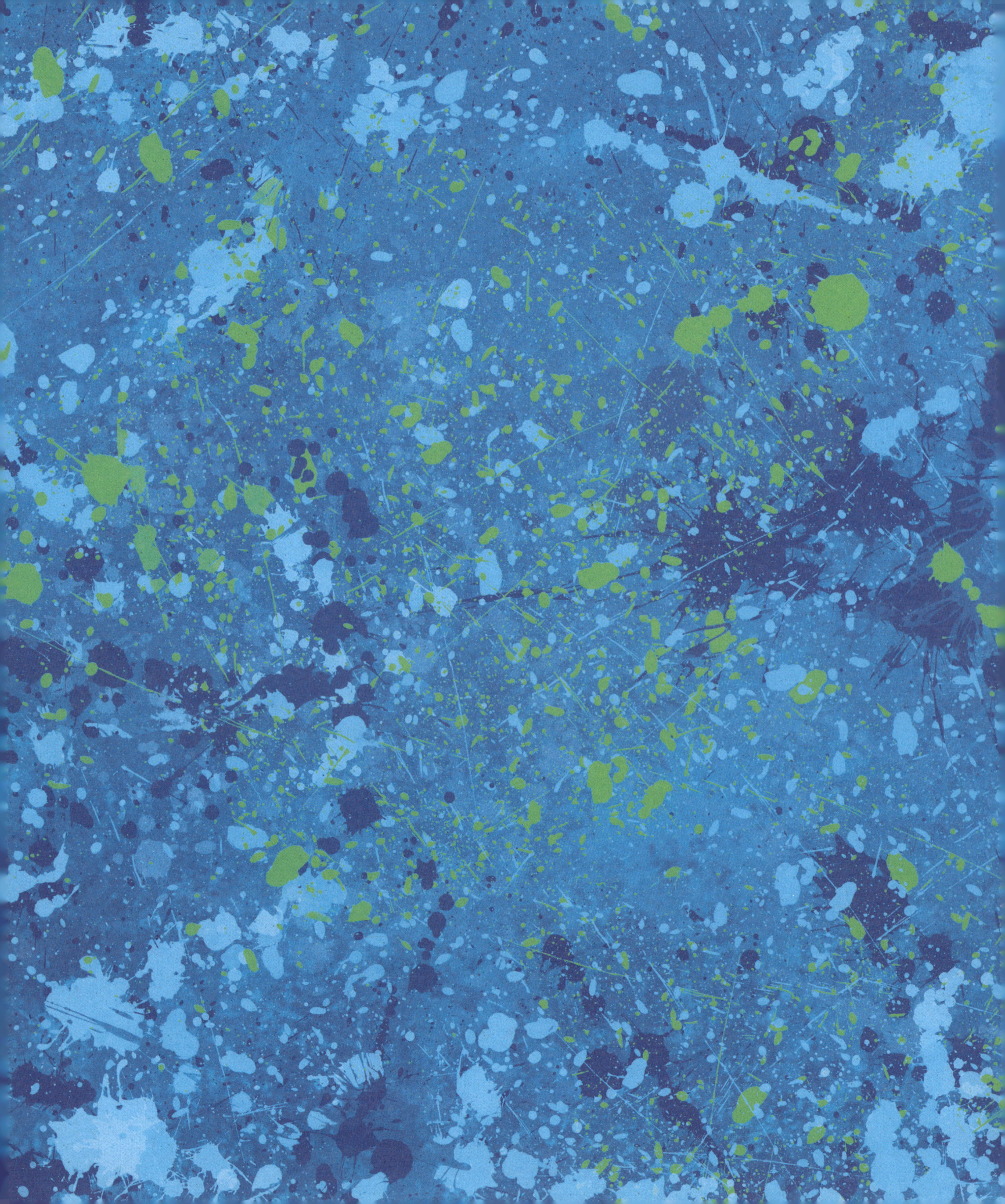